Respect.

Book Of Dhi Peace By Abhi DhiYogi

NABROS & Partners LLC First Edition
April 2026.

Special discounts are available for education and in-need institutes plus bulk orders. An author event/concert may be requested. For permission and all other requests please contact:

NABROS & Partners LLC., 4320 Winfield Rd: Suite 200, Warrenville, IL-60555, USA | iINVENTme.org | Email: hello@nabros.com | Phone: +1 630 796 7676

Printed and created in the United States of America. Library of Congress Cataloging-in-Publication Data is available.

Print ISBN: 978-1-963651-04-1

Ebook ISBN: 978-1-963651-05-8

# CONTENT


Introduction
Page 1-4


Ideas 325 to 432
Page 5-117


Credits
Page 118

# THANK YOU

To the family I have,
and the strangers I met along the way.
To each good experience,
And the bad ones that led me a stray.
To my friends who were there when in
need,
And to those who showed me my weak
knees.
To the happy memories,
And to the sad ones that made sure I
don't forget.
To the Mother of all,
And to the Father I will meet one day.
I thank all of you for
the adventure of circles and the infinite
moments in which we finally intersect.

Dec 7 2014  1 pm  @1816zenden

# ABOUT

Dhi is the essence within each one, which
resonates with…
This resonance of ideas is
a manifestation to compliment one's
unique journey of life, love and light
with Dhi Yoga:
Balance in everything to catch
ideas.
Open up to all to plant the ideas.
Learn the lesson in each
experience, be it good or bad, to
grow the ideas.

A good idea is one which helps self,
others and nature.

If fish are special because they have fins
and birds are special because they have
wings, us humans, we have the intellect to
manifest ideas as our core strength.

Oct 16 2016  6 pm  @1816zenden

# A LETTER TO DHI

"As you embark on this journey called life,
Remember, you do not have to
become anyone.
You were born a masterpiece,
You are the best and there is no one
else like you.
Taking one opportunity at a time
along the way,
Whenever you give your best,
That best in you will be
realized, little by little.
And with each choice made,
You may face a resulting win
or loss, good or bad, yes or a no…

But, learning and sharing the lesson
in each experience,
Irrespective of the result, will lead you to
the best this life has to offer.
Wishing you give the best and learn from
the rest as you embark on this journey
called life."


May 22 2018  2 pm  @1816zenden

IDEA:

Where is the "Peace", within or outside?

If everything that is born passes
away one day,
Then does everything that passes
away take birth some day?


DHI-325
Nov 15 2018  1 pm  @1816zenden

Incorrect practice of mindfulness or
spirituality may lead to an addiction of
"no thinking" and making the mind lazy.
Balance is the key.


DHI-326
Dec 4 2018  1 pm  @1816zenden

I wish
for a mind like the Earth,
with her balanced seasons.
I wish
for a heart like the Sun,
who keeps on giving.
I wish
for a breath like the Space,
which is aware of everything in play.

DHI-327
Dec 8 2018  11 am  @1816zenden

May be:
To the age of 20 I grows with the mind
and body.
To the age of 40 I creates with the heart
and mind.
To the age of 60 I becomes aware with
the breath.
After 60 I starts to be conscious of the
truth in life.

DHI-328
Dec 11 2018  6 pm  @1816zenden

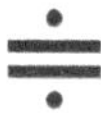

Planets, stars, sun, moon and everything sprouted in space. One day when the time is up, they will merge back into space.
If everything sprouts from love and merges into love, then is space filled with love?


DHI-329
Dec 14 2018  6 am  @1816zenden

Each being born on this planet is made
up of the 5 elements at the core: water,
earth, light, air and space. And again
merges back into those elements when
time is up.
Space being the key element - full of love.

DHI-330
Dec 16 2018  12 pm  @1816zenden

When all is read,
When all is thought,
When all is felt,
When all is said and done,
My love yearns to merge with
The Beloved.


DHI-331
Dec 18 2018  8 am  @1816zenden

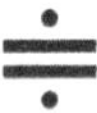

When you merge in love,
only to realize the truth:
What makes love tick
has always been within you.


DHI-332
Dec 22 2018  11 am  @1816zenden

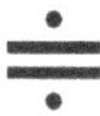

Mind Heart and Breath,
Ideas Love and Truth,
Balance, Open and Learn,
Give, Sacrifice and Pray:
They all make perfect sense as their
essence comes forth in Dhi.

DHI-333
Dec 24  2018  1203 am  @1816zenden

Where will I want to go
when I reach my destiny?


DHI-334
Dec 24 2018  12 pm  @1816zenden

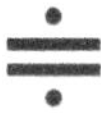

One could be right next to someone and
feel a gap of million miles in between.
And there could be someone who may be
thousands of miles away and one may
feel right next to them.
Space and time, I tell you is a mystery.

DHI-335
Dec 24  2018  2 pm  @1816zenden

If I am able to give my best to someone
and accept whatever may come my way,
then am I in love with that one?


DHI-336
Dec 25  2018  9 am  @1816zenden

# Does commonsense hide in awareness?

DHI-337
Dec 27  2018  11 am  @1816zenden

It is the knowledge gained in awareness
that carries us forward transcending the
dimensions of space and time.

DHI-338
Dec 27 2018  12 pm  @1816zenden

Love sprouts in each moment when one
gives the best and accepts the rest.


DHI-339
Dec 28 2018  2 pm  @1816zenden

As I reflect on the ups and downs,
wins n' losses, smiles n' tears of the year
gone by,
Only a feeling of gratitude comes forth.
For I realize, each one of the
experiences
was always a blessing
to enable me become better
than who I was last year.

DHI-340
Jan 1  2019  11 am  @1816zenden

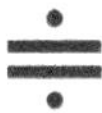

How to solve any problem or challenge at school, work or home:

First, write down the problem statement and underline key info.

Then write the information, logic/formula(s) or choice(s) you think that can be applied to solve the problem.

Finally, start working on the solution.

DHI-341
Jan 3 2019  9 am  @1816zenden

The anger from frustrations and
disappointments sometimes may
become over bearing.

A practice that may help in such a
situation for one to find peace:

Acknowledge I am angry.
Accept that I am angry.
Become aware I am Angry.

In this light, one may find the true
nature of anger.

DHI-342
Jan 4 2019  11 am  @1816zenden

Sadness, frustrations, disappointments and heart breaks may result in one going around in circles with the same thoughts and feelings.

A practice that may help in such a situation for one to find peace:

Acknowledge I am sad.
Accept that I am sad.
Become aware I am sad.

In this light, one may find the true nature of sadness or depression.

DHI-343
Jan 4 2019  1103 am  @1816zenden

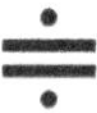

An addiction is a longing and craving
for what one feels is needed and cannot
think of anything else until one has "it".

A practice that may help in such a
situation for one to find peace:

Acknowledge I am addicted to…
Accept that I am addicted to…
Become aware I am addicted to…

In this light, one may find the true
nature of one's addictions.

DHI-344
Jan 4 2019  1105 am  @1816zenden

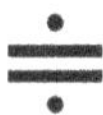

The so called Gurus found out one comprehends the truth from one's breath. And they wrote all about how breath and meditation is the path to the truth, and they claim, everything else in this life is just an illusion.

Dhi Perception:

Truth is in everything: you, me, air, water and all around. With each breath we manifest this truth in the form of love in our heart and ideas in our mind to color this world as it was meant to be.

So what am I to do?

Give the best and accept whatever Dhi gets, to witness the magic in each breath.

DHI-345
Jan 6 2019  7 am  @1816zenden

If anger and desire are the two sides of the
same coin,
then what is the coin made up of?


DHI-346
Jan 6 2019  11 am  @1816zenden

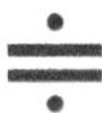

Love is the truth from which all are born
and in which all merge one day.

DHI-347
Jan 7 2019  8 am  @1816zenden

When one gives the best and accepts
whatever comes in return, one
experiences falling in love.

DHI-348
Jan 7 2019  11 am  @1816zenden

Love hides behind each expectation.


DHI-349
Jan 7 2019  11 am  @1816zenden

By opening up and accepting what comes
one's way,
The love in each moment begins to be felt.


DHI-350
Jan 8 2019  9 am  @1816zenden

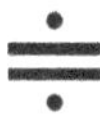

When the stream joins the river,
has it grown to become a river or has the
stream ended?
When the river joins the ocean,
has it merged to become the ocean or did
its life come to an end?
When the sun lifts the ocean and puts it
into the air,
does the ocean die or did it merge with
the air?
When the ocean in the air falls as rain
drops into the  stream below,
did the ocean become a stream?

DHI-351
Jan 14 2019  10 pm  @1816zenden

The best within each one is
manifesting in each breath.
The question is:
Is one awake or a sleep?

DHI-352
Jan 16 2019  9 pm  @1816zenden

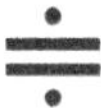

Mind takes Dhi surfing on the waves of
thoughts, feelings desires, ideas, fears…
the list goes on.

DHI-353
Jan 17 2019  1 pm  @1816zenden

Heart takes Dhi surfing on the waves of
love, purpose, choice, relationships…and
the list goes on.


DHI-354
Jan 17 2019  1 pm  @1816zenden

When all that One needs is the breath,
why does Dhi go looking for something
else?"

DHI-355
Apr 10 2019  1 pm  @1816zenden

All that one is seeking in life is right
under the nose..in the breath.


DHI-356
Apr 10 2019  1 pm  @1816zenden

"Life is in the Breath. Breath is in the life."

DHI-357
Apr 10 2019  1 pm  @1816zenden | From a conversation with Bapu

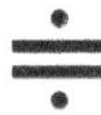

I came here riding on the Breath.
With each in and out, I was mesmerized
with what I saw, heard, scented, felt
and tasted.
This familiar place became my world,
Forgetting the home I had come from.
Over the days, weeks, years and ages,
As i started to get bored,
I grew more inquisitive to find my way
back home.
And I searched, looked and pursued,
I realized who had brought me here in
the first place:
The Breath.
So I tried  to ride on the breath,
Falling off frequently, since I had
forgotten how to ride the wave of the
breath.

Now that I know what to do,
I try in each moment to be with the
breath,
So when the time comes I can ride it
back home.


DHI-358
Apr 14 2019  9 pm  @1816zenden

Ideas in pursuit of peace and happiness
grow into ideas in pursuit of love, which
in turn grow into ideas that pursue truth.

DHI-359
Apr 16 2019  9 pm  @1816zenden

Whatever originates in the mind is driven
by Desires.
Whatever originates in the heart is driven
by Love.
Whatever originates in the breath is
driven by Truth.

DHI-360
Apr 20 2019  1 pm  @1816zenden

# BALANCE

When balanced, we will find our
"Peace" at the center.

When I accept that nothing is mine,
then everything becomes One in peace.

DHI-361
Apr 21 2019  1 pm  @1816zenden

Self and selfless state
are the two faces of the same coin.
By comprehending one
we become aware of the other.


DHI-362
Apr 23 2019  11 pm  @1816zenden

You reflect the best in me.
I hope I reflect the best in you.


DHI-363
Apr 24 2019  1 pm  @1816zenden

Do we find time or do we make time?
Or no need to do anything because we
are given a fixed time?


DHI-364
Apr 26 2019  3 pm  @1816zenden

Time waits for no one except for
The Truth.

DHI-365
Apr 28 2019  10 pm  @1816zenden

Life is a balancing act,
Of the intellect, mind and ego,
Of the time, space and causation,
Of creation, change and maintenance,
Of the positive, negative and neutral,
Of the physical, mental and spiritual
existence,
Of attention, awareness and witness,
Of giving, accepting and learning,
and
Of the One in all and all in the One.

DHI-366
Apr 30 2019  1 pm  @1816zenden
| Modified on Feb 27 2021 9pm

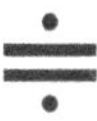

When I has a problem,
Set the veil of ego aside,
And the solution will come to I.


DHI-367
Apr 30 2019  4 pm  @1816zenden

As a kid, I cleaned the room because my
parents said so.
Then I may have cleaned it to please
someone else.
After I had kids, I cleaned it to set an
example.
Then came a day when I cleaned up for
me.
So, now when I clean the room,
I cleans my ideas, thoughts and feelings
within.
In other words,
doing something with a desire graduates
to doing the same out of responsibility
and finally it culminates to giving the best
to what needs to be done to realize the
truth in doing.

DHI-368
May 1 2019  1 pm  @1816zenden

Each of my experiences is just a reflection
of me.


DHI-369
May 1 2019  1 pm  @1816zenden

Behind every successful man there
is a beautiful intelligent woman.
Behind every successful woman
there is an intelligent handsome
man.


DHI-370
May 4 2019  8 am  @1816zenden

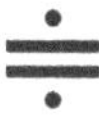

Dhi Mind thought that the
planets and moon go around
the Sun cause of their desire
and need for sunlight.
Then came Dhi hearth with an
understanding that it was love
of Sun which keeps on giving
that may have connected them
all.
Finally, Dhi Breath with the
awareness learnt that the sun,
the moon and planets, all
sprouted from space and what
connects them all is space.
What fills the space is the
peace, love and truth which is
the core existence in each one
of them.

DHI-371
May 6 2019  11 am  @1816zenden

I got on my motorcycle, and started up
the engine.
The intoxicating fumes of gasoline
reached me, as I checked the blinkers and
lights.
I zipped up and slowly crawled through
the sleepy street where everyone had
already moved on to tomorrow.
As I rode, the scent of the October leaves
overwhelmed my being.
Made my left turn after the red,
And then hit the throttle to feel the speed.
As I sped to infinity, everything blurred to
the point of stand still.
Felt as though nothing was moving,
Me, the bike, the wind mills,
All standing still.
Then it dawned like the morning dusk on
me,
Was being perfectly still the fastest I could
be.

DHI-372
May 8 2019  1 am  @1816zenden

One's:
Practice,
Priority,
Perspective
and
Preaching,
Formulates,
The Prayer
Dhi  Pursues.

DHI-373
May 9 2019  12 pm  @1816zenden

"What if" is the fuel for Dhi mind as it
goes round and around the same old
contemplations.


DHI-374
May 10 2019  11 pm  @1816zenden

The only truth One can
tell is about One.
Everything else is just a
perspective,  judgement or
acquired understanding.

DHI-375
May 11 2019  1pm  @1816zenden

Use to think
the trees grew to touch
the stars and the sun.
But now it seems:
The leaves float in the air
and so do the branches.
The water and dust rise up too.
Not in quest of anything higher,
But may be just to float in
Dhi space above
which connects
you, me, birds, trees, leaves…

DHI-376
May 12 2019  11 am  @1816zenden

Whenever I seek truth in anything,
I only tends to find it within.


DHI-377
May 13 2019   1 pm  @1816zenden

Come the night,
The lies put me to bed.
Come the morning,
The truth awakens me to the day.
On one side is Dhi and on the other is I.
As the waves of desires rise,
Love opens its arms,
So all of them may come home,
To the place where they belong.

DHI-378
May 14 2019  8 pm  @1816zenden

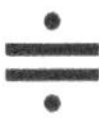

The truth of this existence is in
acceptance of whatever one receives.


DHI-379
May 15 2019  1 pm  @1816zenden

The cosmic intelligence cannot be
processed by a single threaded mind,
but only can be experienced as a
multi-dimensional awareness.


DHI-380
May 18 2019  10 am  @1816zenden

When I look at the self in the mirror and
feel that I have not aged one bit,
I am perceiving the Truth that lies
within.
What connects you and me in an eternal
relationship is Truth,
For everything else breaks with time.
If this is the truth within you and me,
then I guess it must be the Truth within
the sun, sky and the planets plus moon.
Because all of them exist eternally and
connect.
Truth being the core.
Truth being constant. Truth is what
connects me from within to the world
outside.

DHI-381
May 19 2019  11 am  @1816zenden

The first manifestation of expression of
truth is sound, speech or tell the truth.
They don't say think the truth or do the
truth. Thus hypothesizing, the truth
manifesting into this universe first is with
a sound, the big bang.
So as one learns what the mind thinks
and the heart feels, one hopes to
consider this perspective, that our
curiosity is finally driven in seeking truth,
manifesting truth and finally
experiencing the truth.

DHI-382
May 19 2019  11 am  @1816zenden

Life is as good as I is in the here and now.


DHI-383
May 20 2019  8 am  @1816zenden

In your pursuits,
Sometimes you may feel lost.
But turn that corner and you will find
peace my friend.
In your pursuits,
When it may seem you have fallen,
Take a breath and look around,
For you will come to know
that you just fallen in love my friend.
In your pursuits,
When it seems everything is out of your
control,
Turn to your breath,
And the truth in your journey will come
forth my friend.

DHI-384
May 21 2019  11 am  @1816zenden

# OPEN:

In being open and oneself we find our "Peace".

What is life?
Starts with an inhale and ends with
an exhale.
How does life happen?
With an inhale, this world reflects into
us. With an exhale we reflect on to the
world.

Why?
To reflect ideas of the mind, To
reflect the love in the heart. To reflect
the truth within with each breath.

Who am I then?
The one I sees in the mirror who is
ever constant in time.

When can I experience this?
When the mind is balanced and at
peace, the heart is open and in love
and the breath is learning in
awareness.

DHI-385
May 22 2019  1 pm  @1816zenden

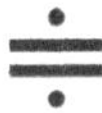

With each breath we reflect onto the
world the ideas our mind is resonating
with, the values our heart is resonating
with and the beliefs our breath is
resonating with.


DHI-386
May 24 2019  3 pm  @1816zenden

One's world is one's own reflection.

DHI-387
May 24 2019  3 pm  @1816zenden

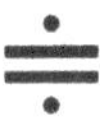

When one is anchored in awareness
resonating with the ideas in the mind,
love in the heart and the truth in breath,
one lives in complete harmony
with the life that manifests.

DHI-388
May 24 2019  3 pm  @1816zenden

In your pursuits,
I wish you peace with each new turn you
take.
If you ever fall,
I wish it is always in Love.
And when you win or gain,
May it be the Truth within each moment.

DHI-389
May 27 2019  1 pm  @1816zenden

Those in positions of power and influence
may believe that they may control human
behavior via information and
manipulation.
But the truth may be:
One's life is designed and driven by the
One who is not bound by time, space and
causation, holding the remote of
consciousness to this self which plays in
the three dimensions of time, space and
causation.

DHI-390
May 28 2019  7 pm  @1816zenden

If I am in love with everyone and everyone
is in love,
Then, where is this Love?


DHI-391
Jun 3 2019  12 pm  @1816zenden

If truth helps my existence, then
am I helping the truth in some way
too?


DHI-392
Jun 3 2019  12 pm  @1816zenden

Does one sense truth or know truth or
become aware of truth?

DHI-393
Jun 3 2019  12 pm  @1816zenden

If I am helping you and you are helping
me and the Truth is helping us,
then who is actually helping who?


DHI-394
Jun 3 2019  12 pm  @1816zenden

When we seem lost my friend,
Pause and take a breath,
For, what we seek will come forth in each
moment.

DHI-395
Jun 15 2019  1 pm  @1816zenden

Love has left behind its foot prints for
those who wish to follow in the path of
peace and harmony.


DHI-396
Jun 15 2019  4 pm  @1816zenden

Love seems to be hiding, in everything,
in everyone, and in each moment.

DHI-397
Jun 15 2019  4 pm  @1816zenden

When things don't go our way,
Reflect,
And Love will help us navigate
the lines of fate.

DHI-398
Jun 15 2019  5 pm  @1816zenden

When the sun goes down,
Love will light the way,
For you and me to reach the
Truth of this journey.


DHI-399
Jun 15 2019  8 pm  @1816zenden

With our dreams we paint this world as it
was meant to be.


DHI-400
Jun 15 2019  8 pm  @1816zenden

We cannot buy time for one self.
So the most precious gift that one can give
to others is to share one's time.


DHI-401
Jun 16 2019  8 pm  @1816zenden

Thank you for making the time to be a
part of my life.


DHI-402
June 20 2019  9 am  @1816zenden

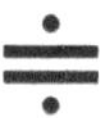

It takes "Two" to make "One".

DHI-403
June 20 2019  1 pm  @1816zenden

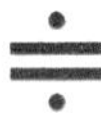

The whole world helps you become
who you really are, as you try to make the
whole world as you are.


DHI-404
June 22 2019  7 pm  @1816zenden

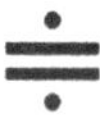

There is truth in everything: good, bad,
happy, sad, attachment, hate, work, play,
birth, death..
How we interpret this truth,
is the life we manifest.
Or in other words:
This life is just a manifestation of one's
interpretation of Truth.

DHI-405
June 24 2019  9 pm  @1816zenden

Does One go with the flow or does
everything flow through One?

DHI-406
June 24 2019  9 pm  @1816zenden

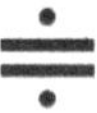

The earth manifested in space.
As it rotates or breathes per se,
does it transform space into what it is
resonating with?


DHI-407
June 26 2019  1 pm  @1816zenden

Does the breathing out cause ripples or waves in the space around one, and they bounce off what is around and return to the one?

DHI-408
June 26 2019  1 pm  @1816zenden

## LEARN:

In peace, we learn the lessons that we need.

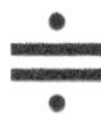

Today, the process of learning is:
Formal education first,
Life lessons second.
Commonsense and values comes third.

The priority of learning should be:
Commonsense and values should come
first.
Life lessons second.
Formal education third.

DHI-409
June 27 2019  3 pm  @1816zenden

The practice of just watching the breath
should be taught as a primary skill to all,
not to change the pace of it, but to just
watch the breath.

DHI-410
June 27 2019  3 pm  @1816zenden

Sometimes I loose my self in happiness,
and sometimes in sadness.
Sometimes I loose my self in anger
and sometime in desire.
Sometimes I loose my self in the company
of others, or when meditating alone.
But when I becomes aware in the breath,
the self comes back to meet all who are in
the moment that I calls my own.

DIII-411
June 28 2019  11 pm  @1816zenden

As I breath in,
I start from the center and expand in the
space to encompass it.
As I breath out,
I transform the space into what ever I
was resonating with,
and come back to the center.
In the due process of accepting and
giving,
My Dhi may learn the lessons of life.


DHI-412
June 29 2019  12 pm  @1816zenden

Growing up as a kid, I found happiness in the basic needs of food, shelter, play and protection. And in the pursuit of more, I grew up to get a car, money and a home. I was happy for a while when all seemed new. But with time, I pursued more. So I got more cars, more money and a bigger home. Alas, again with time, they all seemed to loose their happiness. One evening, as I walked under the moon, no lingering thoughts or feelings, but just in the moment of walking, I felt the kiss of the breeze on my face. This is what I had seeked, The Peace. Just a blessing that came along on my journey and it had nothing to do with what I had pursued. It had been hiding in every moment waiting for me.

DHI-413
June 30 2019  1 pm  @1816zenden

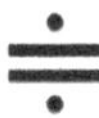

It started with my family then with my friends: the bonding of blood, friendship and love.
In this game of love, as I use to think initially,  it was all about give and take. I did something and expected something in return. The happy moments and the heart aches too. Fascinating.
Then I got married and had kids. And it was this singular act of life, a new born's innocent true love that made me realize love was about giving one's best with no expectations and it was never meant to be a game of give and take.
Come to think of it, Love, true love, was always with me, but  hiding behind the expectation in acceptance of whatever came.

Who put that love behind the expectations my friend?


DHI-414
June 30 2019  1.22 pm  @1816zenden

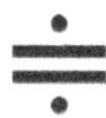

Peaceful and love filled moments were
always disturbed by something or the
someone, unprecedented distractions,
deviations and results.
It was easy to enjoy peaceful moments or
giving the best. But it was really tough to
accept when I got an insult instead of a
thank you from the dear and close ones. I
tried to understand why someone did this
or that which didn't make any sense. But
I just kept going around in circles.
It is when I realized, this life, this
opportunity was about giving the best I
have to each moment but more
importantly, learning to ACCEPT what
ever the moment gave back so I may
learn to do even better in the moments to
come.

DHI-415
June 30 2019  147 pm  @1816zenden

It was a random instance, a moment,
when the picture that was blurred
became a little clear:
This universe was just a reflection of who
I was. And I was just a reflection of the
universe which was filled with Peace,
Love and Truth.
To see the Universe reflect whatever I am
at the moment is easy. But to see I reflect
the peace, love and truth filled universe is
the absolute pursuit.

DHI-416
June 30 2019  158 pm  @1816zenden

Who is "I"?
I am the one constant in time that only I
can see in the mirror.

Where is "I"?
I am in the future, past and present

What is "I"?
I am a circle of life: from the seed to
seed. from the son to father to son. A
never ending circle.

Why is "I"?
I am to manifest peace, love and truth.

DHI-417
June 30 2019  220 pm  @1816zenden

Design of "Dhi":

A triangle with three key points to every level. The Three corners connected via a circle. If one tries to pull away the other two pull it back and in place.

The following examples are the application of the above design. You may apply it to other aspects of your journey.

DHI-418
June 30 2019  220 pm  @1816zenden

Dhi design of Yoga:

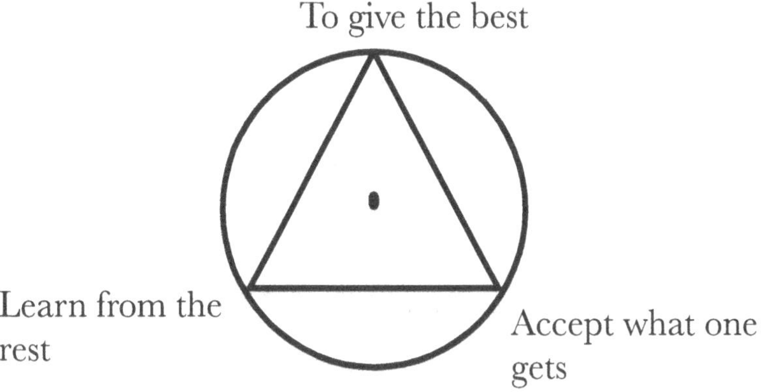


All the three are connected in a triangle. Each one needs the other two. Our life and this universe is the circle. What fills this circle is love. What is at the center is truth.

DHI-419
June 30 2019  225 pm  @1816zenden

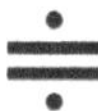

# Dhi design of Consciousness

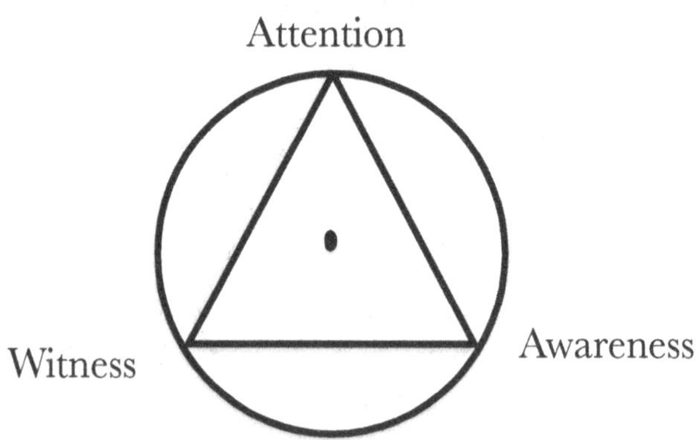


We explore with attention. We learn in awareness. In doing so, we reach the state of being a witness to the miracles.

DHI-420
June 30 2019  228 pm  @1816zenden

# Dhi design of States

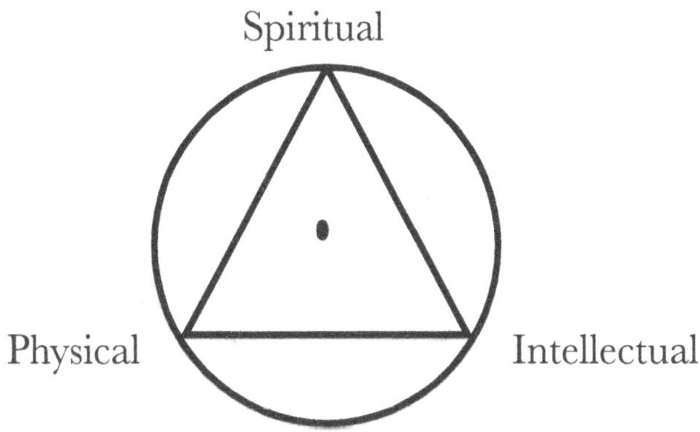


The physical plane is born out of
the intellectual plane. The source
of both starts in the spiritual realm.


DHI-421
Jul 1 2019  1 pm  @1816zenden

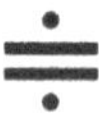

# Dhi design of Breath

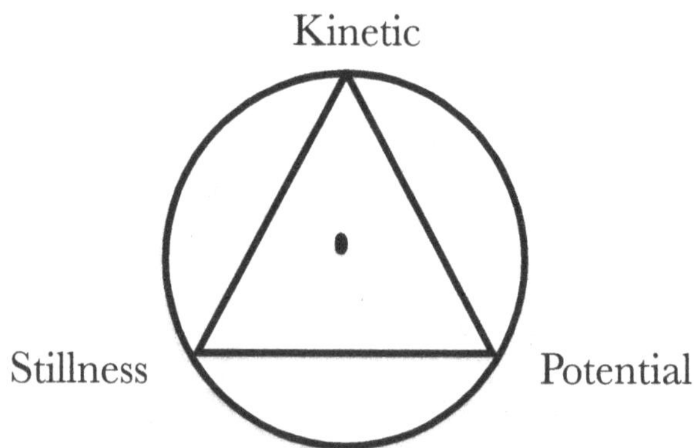


The kinetic part of the breath (vibration) is what
moves within us and in this universe. The small pause
between the inhaled and exhaling breath is the
potential energy. The one who experiences and
observes both is the stillness.


DHI-422
Jul 1  2019  130 pm  @1816zenden

Dhi design of Manifestation:

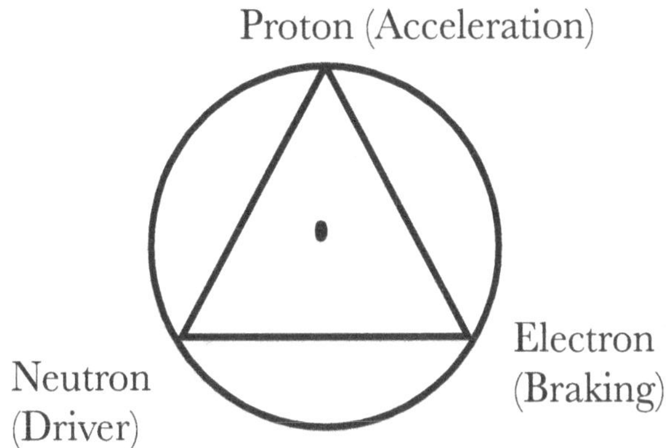


Each and every manifestation, be it our
life, love, light or time or atom, all are
made up of: positive and negative (the
opposites) and the neutral (playground)
in which the opposites play.


DHI-423
Jul 1 2019 140 pm  @1816zenden

## Dhi design of Force:

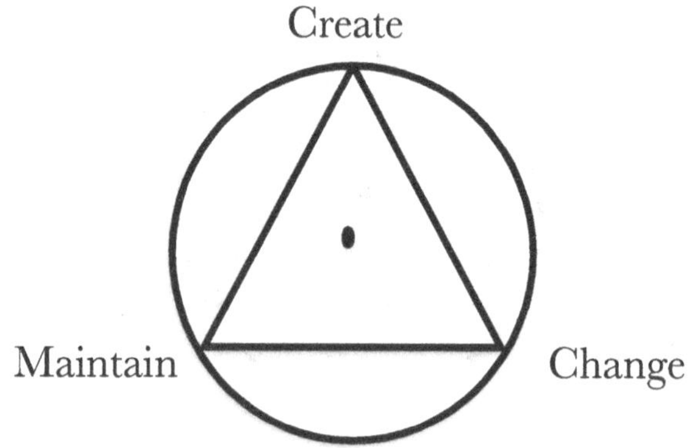


Evolution comprises of creation, changes
and maintaining of the manifestations.

DHI-424
Jul 1  2019 145 pm  @1816zendenn

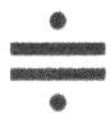

Dhi design of Field:

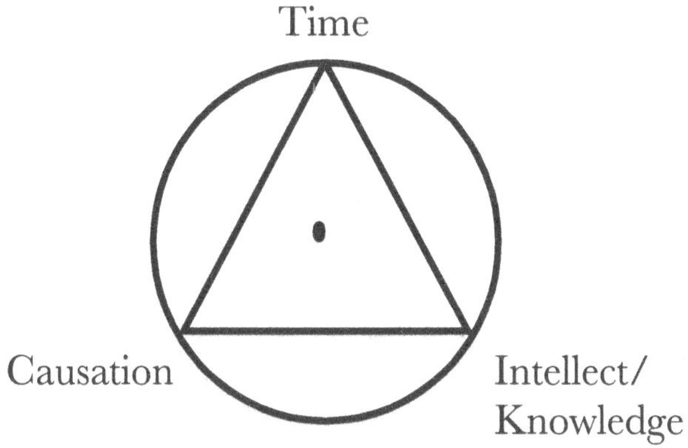


The field within which physical plane
evolves comprises of the time
(frequency), the intelligence or the
knowledge/patterns, and the cause and
effect or causation or karma per se…

DHI-425
Jul 1  2019  2 pm  @1816zenden

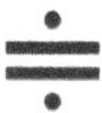

Dhi design of Senses:

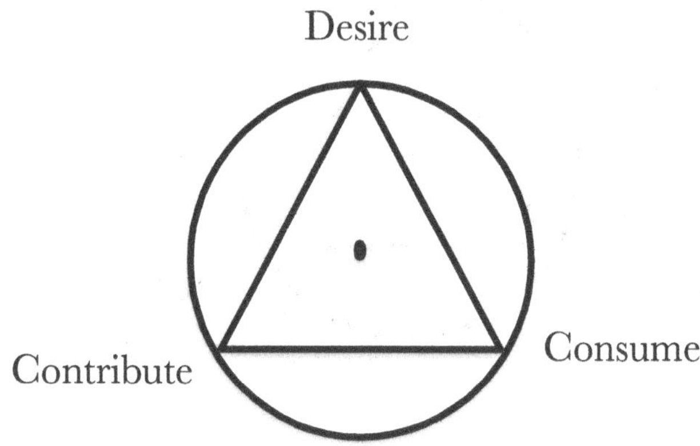


The senses are driven by a desire to
consume or give, contribute per se.

DHI-426
Jul 1 2019  3 pm  @1816zenden

With many I share fun and
experiences.
But only with the One do I
share silence and nothingness.


DHI-427
Jul 9 2019  6 pm  @1816zenden

Does the universe exist as a combination
of 1(something) and 0 (nothing)?


DHI-428
Jul 12  2018  12 pm  @1816zenden

Everything starts with the
breath.
Everything ends in the breath.
Awareness is hidden in the
breath.
The Truth manifests in the
breath.
Breath is the only thing that
goes away when one leaves this
place.


DHI-429
Jul 14 2019  10 pm  @1816zenden

Living in harmony is the
practice that yields peace.


DHI-430
Jul 14 2019  1030 pm  @1816zenden

Do we find peace in love or do we find
love in peace?
Only Truth knows.

DHI-431
Jul 14 2019  1040 pm  @1816zenden

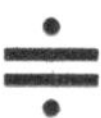

Be it the internal battles,
Or the external wars,
Peace finally wins.


DHI-432
Jul 14 2019  1048 pm  @1816zenden

# DHI CREDITS

Everything in this book, be it the ideas, thoughts, concepts, stories, songs, perspectives and knowledge have been written, sung and communicated by many over the past centuries in their own context.

So what is emphasized in this effort is not original in any form or fashion except from the perspective of Dhi.

Hope we comprehend the words conveyed in their truest essence.

Respect.
Abhi DhiYogi

Oct 16th 2016  6 pm  @1816zenden